W9-CDV-872

T 19464

A Wealth of Wildlife

These very different landscapes are home to very different animals, and animals are an important part of African Mythology.

Different Peoples, Different Myths

In the past, African myths and legends were part of the wide variety of religions that spread across the continent. Each society had its own beliefs with its own gods and heroes.

How Do We Know?

Today, some Africans practice local traditional religions. But most have been influenced by outside beliefs and are now either Christians or Muslims. Ancient African myths and legends survive, often as old stories rather than as living beliefs. Some of these were written down by white missionaries–people who traveled to Africa to convert Africans to Christianity–and explorers in the late 19th and early 20th centuries.

Living Myths in African Art

Many of the characters of African myths and legends survive in African art. African carvings show the gods and peoples of the myths from across the continent. The characters in the illustrations in this book are based on these traditional carvings.

This brightly painted wooden mask was made by the Yoruba of Nigeria. The Yoruba are one of the three main African groups who still hold on to their old beliefs. Masks like this one are used in ceremonies to link dead ancestors with the living.

THE MYTHS & LEGENDS OF AFRICA

The three main African groups who still hold on to their ancient beliefs are the Ashanti of Ghana, the Fon of Benin, and the Yoruba of Nigeria, but records of many myths, legends, and folk tales from all over Africa still survive today.

A MULTITUDE OF MYTHS

Some experts believe that there are over 250,000 African myths and legends, and many thousands of these have been written down and published over the years. The tales chosen for this book are good examples of the themes that come up again and again in African myths and legends.

HOME OF THE SPIRITS

Throughout Africa many people believed that the forest and bush were home to gods and spirits. In a continent where resources are still scarce and much of the land is desert, the forest and the bush could provide both food and shelter—so what better place for a god or spirit to live?

This map shows the borders of the many countries of Africa and the homelands of the ancient Ashanti, Fon, and Yoruba peoples.

MEDITERRANEAN SEA

RED SEA

BENIN

NIGERIA

GHANA

INDIAN OCEAN

ATLANTIC OCEAN

Home of the Ashanti
Home of the Fon
Home of the Yoruba

MYTH OR LEGEND?

Long before people could read or write, stories were passed on by word of mouth. Every time they were told, they changed a little, with a new character added here and a twist to the plot there. From these ever-changing tales, myths and legends were born.

WHAT IS A MYTH?

In early times, people developed stories to explain local customs and natural phenomena, including how the world and humanity developed. These myths were considered sacred and true. Most include superhuman beings with special powers.

WHAT IS A LEGEND?

A legend is very much like a myth. The difference is that a legend is often based on an event that really happened or a person who really existed in relatively recent times.

A VAST CONTINENT

Africa is a huge continent, made up of many different peoples in many different countries. Africa covers almost a quarter of all the land on Earth and is about three times bigger than Europe.

A LAND OF CONTRASTS

Africa has a variety of landscapes. Much of it is desert. The Sahara alone measures about 3.5 million square miles. There are tropical forests and grassy plains, too.

This map shows the variety of landscapes in Africa.

rain forest
mountains
grasslands
deserts

MEDITERRANEAN SEA

SAHARA

RED SEA

NAMIB DESERT

KALAHARI DESERT

ATLANTIC OCEAN

INDIAN OCEAN

World Book Myths & Legends Series

AFRICAN MYTHS & LEGENDS

AS TOLD BY PHILIP ARDAGH

ILLUSTRATED BY GEORGIA PETERS

World Book, Inc.
a Scott Fetzer company
Chicago

Trickster Animals

Animals are an important part of African myths, legends, and folklore. One of the reasons for this is that Africa is home to such a wide variety of creatures, from ants to elephants. Some of the most common animal myths involve a "trickster." The trickster animal lives by its wits and fools its enemies and friends alike. It is usually a hare, frog, spider, or tortoise, depending on which part of Africa the myth comes from.

Passed on by Slaves

Many African myths and legends, those involving trickster animals, traveled to the Caribbean and across North America. This happened because of the slave trade, when Africans were taken abroad against their will and forced to work for no pay. These African myths changed as they were retold by the slaves of North America and the Caribbean and were adapted to fit this new life far away from home.

When stories of the African trickster hare reached North America, the character became Brer Rabbit, the hero of many African American tales.

Note from the Author

Myths and legends from different cultures were told in very different ways. This book aims to tell new versions of these old African tales, not to try to copy the way in which they were first told. On the following pages you will find a mixture of African myths and legends–some exciting, some funny, and some sad. I hope that you enjoy them and that this book will make you want to find out more about Africa and its myths and legends.

5

THE CHALLENGE AND THE MESSENGER

According to the myths of some Nigerian peoples, Olodumare is the supreme god. His name means "great everlasting majesty." But according to a Yoruba myth, there was a time when Olokun, the god of water, wanted that title for himself.

"I'm tired of doing Olodumare's bidding," said Olokun one day, as he walked along the banks of the river that bore his name, his human servant at his side. "Am I not one of the most loved and worshiped gods? Does my river not fill the oceans of the world and bring water to every plant, every animal, and every human?"

"Oh, yes, mighty Olokun," said the servant.

The god and his servant stopped and looked across the river—which was also known as the Ethiope—to the land of the souls. This is where the souls of the dead come to rest and the souls of newborn babies begin their journey into the world.

"Am I not the giver of life?" asked Olokun.

Just then the soul of a child about to be born in a nearby village crossed the river and stopped before the water god. He blessed the soul with secret, sacred words and sent it on its journey full of hope for the new life it was about to begin.

"You are the most loved and respected god of all," said his servant, bowing before him. "Your temples are the most colorful. They are filled with the finest fabrics and the most beautifully carved statues. There are shrines to you in many houses, and you are worshiped every day."

JAMES RIVER ELEMENTARY MEDIA CENTER

"Enough!" cried Olokun. "All that you say is true, yet Olodumare is the most honored. He is still supreme god . . . lord and master of us all!"

Olokun returned to his palace under the sea, wondering how he could challenge Olodumare for supremacy. Olokun was a good and kind god. He was usually wise and generous and used his powers without harming humans . . . but the one thing that caused a look of anger to cross his handsome face was Olodumare's respected position.

Olokun's underwater palace was truly splendid—filled with beautiful things to admire and enjoy. It was a magical place and included a treasure house full of gifts to give to humankind. This fantastic storeroom was no longer as full as it used to be, for Olokun had shared many gifts with the people.

"What has Olodumare ever done for humankind, apart from control people's lives?" sighed Olokun. "Lives which I help to make bearable and even beautiful. Is it not I who make women beautiful? Is it not I who give humans the children they long for and the good luck they deserve?"

At that moment the halls of the palace were filled with the sound of sweet singing, and a row of dancers appeared before the god.

"What can Olodumare offer that I cannot?"

"I can think of little," said the servant.

"Little?" said Olokun.

"I mean nothing," the servant added quickly. "I can think of nothing."

"Then I shall challenge Olodumare for supremacy. Let us see who is fit to be the god of gods!" cried Olokun, and with that thought in mind, he settled back to enjoy the rest of the dance.

So Olokun sent his servant to Olodumare to deliver a message to the supreme god, and the servant was more than a little afraid.

Olokun's servant trembled before the god.

"Why have you come here?" asked Olodumare. "Why are you so afraid of me?"

"You know why, great Owner of Heaven," said the servant.

"Do I?" asked Olodumare, leaning forward on his enormous throne.

"You know everything and hear everything," said the servant.

"Tell me why you are here, all the same," said the supreme god.

"My master, Olokun, challenges you for the right to become the great everlasting majesty," said the servant, his mouth dry with fear.

"Do you think he will succeed in his challenge?" smiled Olodumare.

"It is not for me to say," said the servant, his eyes fixed to the ground.

"A wise answer," said the god. "I admire your loyalty to Olokun, but can't you see that your master is doomed to fail?"

"He must think otherwise," said the servant.

"How high and mighty of him!" laughed Olodumare. "Olokun is usually such a level-headed god. He must really want my position. . . . Tell him I accept his challenge."

Olokun's servant was amazed. "You *accept*, Creator?" he gasped. "Olokun may come here and challenge you?"

Olodumare slowly rose to his feet. "Did I say that?" he smiled. "I said that I accept the challenge, nothing more. Of course, I am far too busy to meet Olokun's challenge myself. I have far more important things to spend my time on than putting jealous gods in their place. . . . Tell your master that I will send a messenger to meet his challenge."

He won't like that, thought the servant.

"He'll have to like it," said the supreme god, reading the servant's thoughts. "Olokun must treat the messenger with as much respect as if I myself were there. Now go and tell your master to prepare for my messenger's arrival."

"A messenger?" Olokun bellowed when he heard the news. "I challenge Olodumare for the right to take his place, and he sends a messenger?"

"An important messenger," said the servant. "So important that Olodumare insists that you treat him with the same respect you would him."

"Very well," said Olokun. "Perhaps Olodumare grows old. He knows I will beat him in any challenge, so he cannot bear to face me."

Wisely the servant said nothing.

"All I can do now is wait," said Olokun. He clapped his hands together. "Let there be music and dancing!" he ordered.

Suddenly there was a commotion in the undersea palace. News reached Olokun's ears that the messenger had arrived.

"He is here already?" said Olokun to his servant. "Let me change my robes, and then I will meet him." So the servant showed the messenger to a seat and waited for Olokun's return.

His master made a grand entrance, his newest robes swishing and swirling around him like the waves of the sea above. Who could fail to be impressed by such fine clothes?

Olokun's jaw dropped open in surprise when he saw the messenger, who had politely got to his feet on Olokun's arrival. The messenger was wearing exactly the same clothes as he! Olokun had worn his newest robes to show just how important he was, only to find that this lowly messenger was equally well dressed!

"Excuse me while I go and change out of these old rags," said Olokun. He left the room and hurried back to his chamber to search for even finer clothes.

Dressed in beautiful finery and color, Olokun soon returned to the messenger. As he swept across the floor, every servant, every dancer, and every singer he passed gasped at the beauty of his garments. They had never seen their god master look so magnificent . . . but the messenger's clothes again matched his!

Seething with anger, but fighting to hide it, Olokun addressed Olodumare's messenger a second time. "Forgive me," he said. "I appear to have a speck of dirt on this, my least favorite robe. Let me change once more, and then I shall join you."

Fuming with rage, he hurried back to his chamber and put on the finest clothing he possessed—the very robes that he had been planning to wear once he had defeated Olodumare and taken the title of supreme god.

No messenger could ever have dreamed such beautiful clothes existed. This would stun even Olodumare's most expert messenger. . . .

But Olokun was wrong. When he returned, the messenger's clothes again matched the god's finery. Olokun felt deflated and defeated. How could he ever hope to challenge Olodumare himself when his mere messenger could match his every move?

Suddenly Olokun realized how foolish he had been. Why couldn't he be happy being the most loved and respected of the gods? He brought children and beauty to the world. He had no need to be the most honored god, or the supreme one.

He put his hand on the messenger's shoulder. "Go back to Olodumare and tell him I have learned my lesson," he said quietly. "Tell him that you have defeated me before the challenge has even begun."

Without having spoken a word, the messenger left Olokun's undersea palace and returned to the heavens.

Olokun never knew it, but he had been tricked by nature. The messenger was a chameleon—an animal that can change its color and markings to blend in with its surroundings. It had blended in with Olokun's clothing and matched it robe for robe.

THE BATTLE WITH DEATH

Rain can be a matter of life and death in South Africa. Without it crops shrivel up and die, leaving people with little or no food. This story, based on a myth of the Khoi people, tells of one man's fight to save his starving tribe.

Long ago, when a terrible famine plagued the land, there lived a man whose birthname has long since been forgotten. He became known as Tsui'goab, but that was not his name when our story began.

Tsui'goab was worried for the future of his village. "Will the rain never come?" he sighed, blinking in the brilliant sunshine as he looked in despair for a cloud in the clear blue sky. "Most of our cattle have died, our crops cannot grow, and more people die of thirst and hunger by the day. Will it never end?"

Of all the wells within walking distance, there was only one that had not dried up, and no one knew how long this one would last. Every day the bucket went lower and lower into the ground before it reached the water.

But how should the villagers use this precious supply? If they drank it themselves, the few cattle they had left would die. If they gave it to the cattle, they wouldn't be able to water the crops. Without cattle or crops there would be no food, and without water for themselves, they too would be dead in a matter of days.

Looking up at the sun in the sky, Tsui'goab wondered how something so beautiful could be so deadly. . . .

The sun was a friend. It brought warmth and light and gave plants the energy to grow. But it could also be an enemy. It brought death to the land. Without any rainfall the sun scorched the earth, making a plot of farmland as dry as dust.

Then one day a traveler came to the village. He stood in the house of one of the elders. Drought or no drought, strangers were still made welcome. Although the traveler's head was covered with a hood and his body was hidden by robes, Tsui'goab–who, remember, wasn't called Tsui'goab in those days–could tell that this was a healthy being. His arms and legs were muscular, no bones showed through his skin, and unlike Tsui'goab and the other villagers, his skin did not look cracked and dry.

"Have you come a long way?" asked Tsui'goab.

"Near and far," said the traveler.

"Is the drought widespread? Did you see much death along the way?" asked Tsui'goab.

"There was death wherever I went," said the traveler.

"But from what little I can see of you, you yourself look so healthy," said Tsui'goab. "What is your secret?"

"Secret?" said the traveler. "What do you mean?"

"I think you know what I mean," said Tsui'goab, his eyes narrowing in the dark of the house. "Have you ever been to our village before?"

"Yes and no," said the hooded traveler, his voice barely a whisper.

"Throw off your hood," said Tsui'goab. "There's no need to hide your face. Small wonder that you say you are from near and far–for death is everywhere. Small wonder that you say there was death wherever you went–for you *are* Death."

The traveler threw off his cloak and hood. "Yes, I am Gaunab," he said. "Some think of me as Death."

"And I am glad you are here in human form," said Tsui'goab, at last seeing that there might be something he could do to try to save his people.

"Glad?" grinned Gaunab. "I think your lack of food and water is affecting your thinking."

"Not at all," said Tsui'goab. "My people are a proud people. We are not afraid to stare Death in the face, but it is not often that you show us a *human* face."

"Is my face handsome?" asked Gaunab.

"Yours is the face of empty, swollen bellies, of dry, cracked lips and swarms of flies," said Tsui'goab. "It is a face of burning sun and dried-up watering holes. How can that be handsome?"

"You're not afraid of me, are you?" said Gaunab.

"No," said Tsui'goab. "If you hadn't come here in human form I would have called out to you."

"You want to die?" said Gaunab. "I don't believe you. You care too much for those around you to want that."

"What I want is to challenge you to a fight," said Tsui'goab. "A fair and honest fight, which if I win will mean that you promise to go away from here forever and leave my people alone."

"You want to banish me?" said Gaunab. "You want to banish *Death*?"

"Yes," said Tsui'goab.

"And what if you lose?" said Gaunab at last.

"Then you take my life and the lives of all those around us," said Tsui'goab quietly.

"That's not much of a prize, seeing as I shall soon have all your lives anyway," said Gaunab.

"So you will not meet my challenge and fight me?" asked Tsui'goab.

"Do you trust me to fight fairly?" asked Gaunab.

"Yes," said Tsui'goab.

"Why?" asked Gaunab.

"Because you are Death, and the only opposite to death is life. You are what you are," said Tsui'goab. "There is honesty in that. You cannot be something in between."

"Then I accept your challenge!" said Gaunab.

Before Tsui'goab had a chance to prepare himself, Gaunab jumped at him, and they rolled, wrestling, out into the blazing sunlight.

Soon the news had spread around the village. "Tsui'goab is fighting with Death himself!" the villagers cried—though, of course, they didn't call him Tsui'goab because that wasn't his name back then.

The sick and the dying were carried out of their homes by the more healthy, though no one was really fit and well in such as dreadful drought. Every villager who had the strength joined in the shouts and cheers of encouragement to Tsui'goab as he wrestled with Death. They knew that he was fighting for their lives as well as his own.

Gaunab and Tsui'goab seemed quite closely matched. Gaunab was fitter, but Tsui'goab was quicker on his feet and seemed to know more tricks. The fight seemed to go one way and then the other. . . .

But Tsui'goab had more to fight for. As he wrestled with Death, he remembered the loved ones whom Death had taken from him in his life and thought of those who would die if he failed. This gave him the strength to carry on when he might otherwise have given up.

No one can recall how long the fight lasted. Some say many hours, but others say many days. There are even those who say that it lasted weeks. One thing is for sure, though, and that is the outcome. After a momentous struggle, Gaunab finally crashed to the dusty ground and didn't get up.

"I'm dying," he said, a look of utter amazement on his face. "You have defeated Death."

Tsui'goab, exhausted and streaked with dirt and blood, stumbled over to his opponent. "This was only possible because you were honorable and fought fairly," he said. "I—"

But Gaunab was not yet finished. His last act was to lash out at Tsui'goab, shattering his kneecap with an awful CRUNCH. Tsui'goab screamed and toppled over in terrible pain. Then there was blackness.

When Tsui'goab awoke, he heard voices but did not open his eyes right away. He felt very strange.

"Tsui'goab may have defeated Gaunab," said a voice, "but Death takes many forms and still stalks the earth."

"But Tsui'goab has saved his people this time," said another.

Tsui'goab wondered who this "Tsui'goab" was they were talking about, because he didn't yet know that he'd been given a new name.

"No other human has ever wrestled with Death in such a way before," said the first voice. "He has proved his worth, and now, with the gifts we have given him, he can save his people."

Tsui'goab opened his eyes. He was alone, but understood what he had heard, for he was not lying on a bed or on solid ground, but in the sky. He could see his village far below him. He stretched his arms out with new-found strength, and as he brought his hands down to his sides, rain poured from his fingers.

He watched in joy and wonder as the color of the soil down below turned darker and darker as it soaked up the rain–rain that he himself had created. He watched the villagers–*his* villagers–run from their houses and lift their faces to the skies. His people were saved!

Tsui'goab had become a rain god, with a new home in the skies. New gods need new names, which is how he came to be called Tsui'goab. It means "wounded knee."

How the Animals Came

According to an old myth of the Dogon people of Mali, the world was created by the god Amma. Amma put people on the earth . . . but how did the animals come?

Amma, the creator, made the world. First he took a giant pot of clay, which he fired in an oven until it was white-hot. Then he wrapped it in red copper and cast it into the sky, bringing light.

"You are my sun," he said.

Next he took a smaller pot, fired it in his oven, then wrapped it in white copper–which we now know as brass–and threw it into the other corner of the sky.

"You are my moon," he said.

Then he broke off a piece of the sun, shattered it into a thousand pieces, and scattered it across the heavens. "You are my stars," he said.

Then he took some clay and created the earth. "You are Mother Earth, my wife," he said. "From you our children will grow." With that he caused the first downpour of rain on earth, and twins were born from the soil.

The twins looked very much like the humans that Amma was later to create, but each had the tongue of a lizard and the tail of a snake. These were Amma's first children—Water and Light.

Water and Light joined their father in the heavens and looked down on their beautiful mother, the earth.

"She has no clothes!" said Light.

"Then we must clothe her," said Water.

Together Water and Light made green grass grow and plants sprout up to cover their mother's nakedness. It is the same today–plants need water and light to grow.

Now Amma, the creator, modeled First Man and First Woman out of clay, set them on the earth, and breathed life into them. Soon they in turn had eight children–two sets of male twins and two sets of female twins–and these were the first Dogon people.

Once again Water and Light looked down on Mother Earth, now covered in green, and decided that she needed more clothes.

"What are you doing?" asked Amma, their father.

"We are weaving Mother a skirt of reeds and shrubs, which we will clothe her with," they explained, as their father sat beside them in the heavens. All three talked together as Water and Light made the skirt.

What none of them realized was that the twisting of reeds and wrapping of leaves was creating a wind, which blew their words down to the surface of the earth. Here the words were heard by the people, and because they were spoken by the gods, the people understood them. They started speaking to one another, and this was how human language was born.

Amma, Water, and Light looked contentedly around their new world.

"It is done," said Amma. "My people are happy."

"But the earth is so large," said Light. "Couldn't she have more people to care for?"

So their father took some shining sunlight and created the shining black people of the world. He then took a piece of pale moonlight and created paler-skinned people, and placed the peoples on Mother Earth.

"Now your work is finished, Father," said Water. "You have created a beautiful world." All three went to the heavens to rest.

The first people loved their home. They loved the bright sun in the morning sky and the moon at night.

They loved the plants and trees and the earth beneath their feet. They loved the rains from the heavens. And they loved the language they had caught on the winds and could use to talk to one another.

"Our creator is a wise and generous god," said a young man, "but there are words in our language for things I've never seen. What are these animals he spoke of? There are so many different words for them. If only we could see such wondrous beasts!"

"But if they're not on earth, where can these animals be?" asked the woman.

"Why, in the home of Amma himself, of course," said the man. "These animals must live in the heavens. We should ask him to send some down to us."

The young woman laughed. "If the creator had wanted us to share Mother Earth with animals, he would have put them here with us."

The young man nodded. "Then we will have to go up to the heavens and steal them!" he said triumphantly.

It was agreed that a small band of people would climb up to the heavens and take one male and one female of each animal.

"How will we bring them back?" asked one.

"We will build a giant wooden pyramid," said the young man. "We don't know the size of these animals, but we can put the largest at the bottom and the smallest at the top."

"And how will we get the pyramid back down to earth once it is full?" asked another.

"We will lower it with thick rope," said the young woman.

"You've thought of everything!" cried one.

"Then let's set to work!" said another.

When the pyramid was ready, the team of people climbed from the highest hill up into the heavens and marveled at the kingdom in the sky. There were giraffes and hippopotamuses, lions and antelope, beetles, birds and fishes, and every other kind of animal you can think of—grazing, running, flying, and swimming above the clouds.

"They're so beautiful!" gasped the young man.

"Shhh!" warned the young woman. "The creator cannot be far from here, and he will not be pleased if he learns that we are here to steal his animals from the heavens."

"Not all of his animals," the young man reminded her. "Just a male and female of each."

So, quickly and quietly, the first Dogon people led the animals into their wooden pyramid, two by two—with the biggest animals at the bottom and the smallest ones on top—until it was full and very heavy.

"There are far more of these animals than I ever imagined," confessed the young man. "We can't lower the pyramid by a rope—it's far too heavy. The rope would snap, and the pyramid would fall to earth. . . ."

"We could push it down there," suggested one, pointing to the beautiful rainbow that joined the heavens and the earth.

"But it would gather speed and still hit the earth with a mighty crash," sighed the young woman. The people were getting restless now, fearful that Amma, Water, or Light might appear at any moment and catch them in the middle of their daring robbery.

"I have it!" said the young man. "We'll lower the pyramid down the rainbow bridge on the rope. Both rainbow and rope together should be enough to take the weight. We will all go ahead of the pyramid to help slow down its descent!"

Everyone agreed, until someone asked, "What shall we tie the other end of the rope to?"

The young man said nothing, but snatched the free end of the rope and tied it to the sun. "Now," he said, "let us take the animals to earth!"

It must have been an amazing and unbelievable sight: a group of people and a giant pyramid, working their way slowly down a dazzling rainbow back to earth.

Imagine how it must have looked to those watching and waiting for their safe return. Imagine their horror when, just as the pyramid safely reached the ground, there was an almighty CRACK.

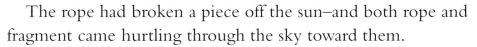

The rope had broken a piece off the sun—and both rope and fragment came hurtling through the sky toward them.

The people scattered as the fragment of the sun hit a bush, which burst into a roaring fire of orange flames. They had never seen flames before and were frightened.

"Amma has done this to punish us!" said a man who had been too afraid to go with the others.

"Nonsense," said the young man. "As well as the animals, we have an extra gift today. See how this fire gives off heat and light. . . . It could be a very useful tool for humankind!" And with that he opened the door of the pyramid, and the pairs of animals came streaming out.

The birds took to the skies; the mammals, insects, and reptiles took to the forests and plains; and the fish took to the water . . . and Mother Earth welcomed them, for she had so much to give.

Up in the heavens Amma, Light, and Water looked down on the earth. "These people I've made are most mischievous creatures," said Amma. "But the animals seem happy in their new world, and your mother nurtures them so well. Now it is their duty to live as one. I'll leave them be . . . for the time being, at least."

THE RACE
TO BE KING

There are many African myths about animals. In some the animals behave like animals. In others they behave like people. And in some myths they are halfway in between. This Alur myth has a frog and a lizard as brother princes.

Lizard and his brother Frog sat staring at each other. Lizard sat in the midday sun, soaking up the heat of the rays. He smiled with contentment. The smooth, black rock beneath him was so lovely and hot that he had to lift each foot in turn. This way all four feet had the chance to cool down a little before getting deliciously hot again on his favorite stone.

Frog stayed in the shade, half in and half out of the water. He liked the damp. He liked to stay cool. If he stayed out in the sun too long, he'd be burned to a crisp.

Frog's big, round eyes were fixed on Lizard. "What are you thinking, Brother?" he asked. "You look very pleased with yourself."

"I was thinking that when our father, the king, dies, I shall take the throne," said Lizard.

"That is up to Father," said Frog, his croaking voice causing tiny ripples in the pool.

"You surely don't think he will choose you to succeed him?" asked Lizard, lifting a back foot off the scalding-hot rock.

"It is his choice," Frog reminded him. "But he grows old and must make the announcement soon."

"I am handsome, fast, and strong," said Lizard, flicking his tongue.

25

"My voice is quiet, yet commanding. You, on the other hand, have none of these qualities," Lizard continued.

"I, like you, am my father's son," said Frog, "and I will stand by his decision, whichever one of us he chooses to be king after him."

"But you are ugly and slimy, *and* you hop!" protested Lizard. "Your croaking voice is crude and loud. You could never be king."

At that moment a messenger arrived. "Prince Lizard," he said with a bow, blinking at the lizard in the brilliant sunlight. "Prince Frog," he added with another bow, squinting into the shade. "Your father summons you both to the royal court."

"To proclaim me his successor, I have no doubt," smiled Lizard.

"His message is that whichever one of you reaches the royal court first is to be king after him," said the messenger, and was gone.

"Hah!" said Lizard, scuttling off his sunning rock with the surprising speed that a lizard has. "I told you, Frog. Father wants me as his successor. I shall be the next king of this land!"

Frog lowered himself right into the water to moisten his skin, then came up for air. "What makes you say that, Brother?" he asked.

"Because I can scuttle and scurry far faster than you can ever hop with your dangly legs and plump body," laughed Lizard. With that he scuttled off into the undergrowth to collect some things for his journey to the royal court.

Frog looked at his own reflection in the pool. His brother Prince Lizard was right. He, a frog, would take far longer to reach the royal court. Lizard would be so determined to reach it first that nothing would stop him.

Nothing, that is, except for a little rain, thought Frog.

As an animal that lived both on land and in water, Frog knew twice as much about the world as his brother Prince Lizard. And that meant that Frog knew twice as much about magic.

Rather than setting off for the race to the royal court—a race he knew he'd lose—Frog went in search of a tree called the yatkot.

Once he'd found the tree, he broke off a twig and ground it into a magical powder, which he then sprinkled into the water. As the frog prince did this, he muttered some secret words, and the spell immediately began to take effect.

First there was a single splash of rain on a large, heart-shaped leaf near him . . . then another . . . and then another. Soon the air was filled with the pitter-patter of rain, and there was a smell of damp soil. Then the heavens opened, and it began to pour down.

"Just the right weather for frogs!" laughed Frog, and he began to hop off in the direction of the royal court.

Meanwhile Lizard was feeling rather proud of himself. He was already well on his way to the royal court.

"I don't know why Father didn't simply announce my name as his successor," he said to himself. "Why go through this pretence of deciding it by a race? Everyone knows that my slimy, green, hop-along brother can never keep up with me—and he'll be burned to a frazzle in this heat."

Just then a large black cloud blotted out the sun, and rain began pouring down. Lizard scuttled under an overhanging rock.

I'll wait here until the rain stops, he thought. It won't last long at this time of year, and I must be so far ahead of Frog that he'll never catch up.

But Lizard was wrong. Frog did catch up, and even overtook him. Of course, Lizard didn't know this, because his brother was traveling by a different route.

At last the rain stopped, and the sun was hot and bright once more —because the magic from a ground yatkot twig can only last for so long before it runs out.

Lizard scuttled out from under his rock and scampered off once more. "I'll soon be at the royal court," he said, then caught sight of himself in a puddle. "What a handsome king I'll make with my fine scales of pretty colors."

Up ahead Prince Frog had reached the gate to the royal court. On the left, in blazing sunshine, stood a row of brightly colored lizards. They were his brother's heralds, ready to greet Lizard's arrival with a fanfare of trumpets. On the right–in the cool shade–stood a row of frogs. These were Frog's heralds. They didn't need trumpets because they had such fine, croaky voices.

On seeing their master arrive, they threw back their heads and croaked a fanfare to announce their prince's arrival and his triumph as winner of the race.

The old king hurried to the gate and greeted his son. "Well done, Frog," he said. "I see you must have used your wits to have won this race, and a good king always needs his wits about him. You will make a fine king when I am dead and gone."

The king's words were drowned out by the lizard heralds' trumpets, announcing Prince Lizard's arrival. Lizard sauntered into the royal court, his head held high.

"Here to greet me, Father?" Lizard asked, somewhat smugly. "I'm sure you'll want to throw a special feast to celebrate my victory. I don't think we should wait for that ugly brother of mine, though. He won't be here for . . . for . . . ."

Lizard stopped. He stared and blinked, then stared again. No, his eyes were not deceiving him. There, in the cool shadows of the royal court, stood his slimy, ugly, hop-along brother. And this could mean only one thing–that his slimy, ugly, hop-along brother had beaten him in the race, and that meant that his slimy . . . That meant that Prince Frog would one day be King Frog.

"Hello, Lizard," said Frog. "What kept you?"

And that is why, whenever you hear a frog chorus, you should be prepared for rain. It means that Frog has passed out of the gates of the royal court and is out weaving his magic with his ground yatkot twigs . . . because you know how much he likes the damp weather!

KIGBO AND THE BUSH SPIRITS

Kigbo was named wisely. His name means "stubborn man," and a stubborn man is one who always wants his own way. According to a Yoruba myth, it was Kigbo's stubbornness that led to all his troubles.

Kigbo and his wife, Dolapo, were both young and had lived with their parents until they were married. This meant that they had no land of their own. When the time came for the villagers to prepare their fields to plant crops, Kigbo's father went to his son's house to see him.

"You have a beautiful wife and a fine son, and now it is time for you to care for them," he said. "Let's find a spot outside the village, clear the ground, and turn it into your very own field."

"No," said Kigbo.

"No?" gasped his father. "But you need to grow crops to feed yourself and your family. You are your own man now, Kigbo. It is not for me or for Dolapo's parents to look after you."

"I meant no to the land just outside the village," said his son stubbornly. "Most of it has been taken, so we'd only be able to clear enough land for a small field."

"But a small field is all you need," his father reasoned. "There is enough land for everyone."

"I want to farm the bush," said Kigbo.

"The bush?" his father gasped. "That is madness. No one farms there. The bush is far away from home, and it is dangerous!"

"I don't mind the distance, and it's *because* no one farms there that I can clear myself the biggest field I want!" grinned Kigbo.

"But the danger–" his father reminded him.

Kigbo looked at his father. "It was you who named me the stubborn one," he said. "You know my mind is made up."

So Kigbo marched off to the bush all on his own. He had just begun to hack away at the undergrowth when a chorus of spirits appeared.

"We are the bush spirits," they said. "This is our land. What are you doing?"

"Clearing a patch to plant my corn," said Kigbo, stubbornly. He wasn't about to let a group of spirits upset his plans.

"We are the bush spirits," the chorus repeated. "This is our land. We do what you do."

So, rather than chasing Kigbo away, the spirits started helping him in his task, and in next to no time, they'd cleared a large area of bush. Satisfied, Kigbo stopped, and the spirits stopped, too. Then, without so much as a "thank you," he headed off back to the village.

Back home, Kigbo's father was waiting with Dolapo outside their house when Kigbo appeared.

"I was so worried about you," she said. "I thought the bush spirits might have caught you and done terrible things to you."

"Terrible things?" laughed Kigbo. "When I started clearing some scrub, they joined in. I got the work done in next to no time. . . . I shall return tomorrow to turn the soil."

"Didn't I teach you anything, you stubborn fool?" said his father. "The bush is a dangerous place, and spirits are not to be trifled with."

When Kigbo returned the following morning, carrying a sack of corn, the chorus of bush spirits appeared once again. "We are the bush spirits. This is our land," they said. "What are you doing?"

"Tilling the soil so that I can plant my seeds," said Kigbo.

"We are the bush spirits," repeated the spirits. "This is our land. We do what you do."

So when Kigbo started breaking up the hard soil that had once been covered by bush, the spirits joined in. In next to no time, the land was tilled and ready for planting. Then he untied the top of the sack, took a handful of grain, and began to sow his crop.

"We are the bush spirits," said the chorus. "This is our land. We do what you do," and they began to sow the grain, too. In next to no time, all the seeds had been planted.

Satisfied, Kigbo stopped and the spirits stopped, too. Then, without so much as a "thank you," he headed off back to the village.

Time passed and the seasons changed. The planting season turned into the growing season, and Kigbo carried on his life in his selfish, stubborn way without a thought for others.

All the other villagers could easily check their small plots just outside the village to see how their corn was growing. Kigbo, however, had to walk all the way to the edge of the bush where he'd cleared his field. But he thought it was worth it. There was a sea of corn glinting in the sunshine. It seemed to stretch forever.

People say I'm stubborn, Kigbo thought, but look how clever I've been. They all have their small plot of land and have to work long and hard at every stage. I have this huge field, and those foolish bush spirits have done most of the hard work for me. When the corn is ripe and ready for harvesting, I expect they will help me again!

Kigbo was so proud of his ripening corn that he decided to fetch his wife and son to show it to them. He set off back to the village.

Dolapo, meanwhile, was feeling guilty. Kigbo may be a stubborn person, she thought, but he is my husband and I love him . . . and when he works, he works very hard. So she decided that she would go out to the bush with their son and see this field for herself.

They must have taken different routes, for their paths did not cross. When Dolapo finally reached the field, there was no sign of Kigbo.

It had been a long walk, and she wished Kigbo wasn't such a stubborn man. Why hadn't he cleared a smaller plot near the village?

Dolapo's little boy started to cry.

"Are you hungry little one?" she asked. "I can't give you any of this corn to eat—it isn't ripe yet."

But her son kept on crying, so Dolapo snapped off a head of corn—even though it wasn't ripe—and gave it to him to eat.

Just then the chorus of bush spirits appeared. "We are the bush spirits," they said. "This is our land. We do what you do," and—before Dolapo knew what was happening—the bush spirits had snapped the heads off *all* the corn. Soon the ground was littered with unripened heads of corn, and the whole crop was ruined!

"What have I done?" cried Dolapo. She sat down and wept. Her cries mingled with those of her wailing baby and became so loud that Kigbo heard them on his journey home. He frowned.

"That sounds like Dolapo and the baby," he said with growing fear. "And it's coming from the bush!"

He turned and ran back to his field as fast as he could. What was Dolapo doing out there with their son? The bush was such a dangerous place. When he arrived at his field, Kigbo was horrified by what he saw. There wasn't a single head of corn left. The field was a useless sea of stalks!

"What happened?" gasped Kigbo.

"Our son was crying with hunger, so I snapped him off a head of corn." his wife explained.

Kigbo then did a terrible thing. He yelled and shook his finger in anger at his son.

Before he had time to realize what was happening the chorus of bush spirits appeared. "We are the bush spirits," they said. "This is our land. We do what you do," and—before he could stop them—they were all shaking their fingers at his poor little son, too.

Kigbo felt guilty and angry about what had happened. It was wrong to treat anyone—least of all a baby—in that way, but he tried to convince himself that it was all Dolapo's fault.

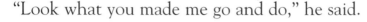

"Look what you made me go and do," he said.

"We are the bush spirits," said the chorus. "This is our land. We do what you do."

Realizing what a stubborn fool he'd been—and the trouble he'd brought to his family—Kigbo began beating his head with his fists.

"I've been such a fool!" he wailed. "Why didn't I listen to my father?"

"We are the bush spirits," said the chorus, turning to him. "This is our land. We do what you do," and they began beating Kigbo.

"This is *our* land," they repeated, but he heard nothing over the blows.

There are many endings to this tale. One says that Kigbo and Dolapo fled the bush with their baby, and Kigbo learned a valuable lesson. Another says that all three of them were killed by the spirits. And a third ending says that Kigbo died at the hands of the spirits and that Dolapo and the boy escaped with their lives.

Whatever may have happened, one thing is for sure. Kigbo's father was right. The bush is a dangerous place, and spirits are not to be trifled with—however helpful they may at first seem.

THE CHILDREN OF THE GOURDS

High on the mountain lived a powerful spirit, who watched over the daily lives of the Chaga people in the valley below. One of the people he became particularly fond of was the Old Widow Woman, who lived all alone.

The village was always filled with the sound of children's laughter, but the Old Widow Woman had no children or grandchildren. Her house was filled with silent sorrow.

When it came to fetching, she had to fetch. When it came to carrying, she had to carry. Water, firewood, supplies, it made no difference—she had to fetch them all herself. In fact, she had only herself for company as she lived out her life the best she could.

When the Old Widow Woman was no more than a girl, she married a fine man, and they were very happy together. But, like many fine men, he died before they had any children, and she swore never to marry again.

There was very little furniture in that tiny house of hers. There were very few belongings, and the whole place looked dusty and unloved. But her fruit and vegetable patch was a different matter. She loved that patch, and every day she would tend her plants in the shade of her neighbor's banana trees. She would weed, water, pick out stones, and shoo away animals. But the plants she was most proud of were her gourds.

The villagers joked about this. "The Old Widow Woman loves those gourds like they were her own children!" they used to say.

Up on his seat in the mountain, the spirit heard every word. He looked down on the Old Widow Woman as he had done every day of her life. He had watched her grow old. He remembered the beautiful young woman she had been on her wedding day—with her straight back and sparkling eyes. Now he saw her bent with age—her eyes dulled and her fingers gnarled. And these were the same fingers that cared for the gourds with such tenderness.

The Old Widow Woman grew her gourds to make into bowls. She left them to dry until the skins hardened, and turned them into bowls called calabashes. She would then sell her calabashes at the market to make what little money she could.

Thinking of the other villagers' jokes and the Old Widow Woman treating her gourds like children, the spirit who lived on the mountain decided that he would help her. He would give the Old Widow Woman real children—magical children—to bring her happiness.

The next day the Old Widow Woman was tending her fruit and vegetable patch as usual when the mountain spirit's messenger appeared behind her. She turned to look at him, but—because he was standing with the sun behind him—she couldn't make out his face. His head was a black silhouette against a dazzling sky.

"And what can I do for you?" she asked.

"Treat the next four gourds you grow with extra care," said the messenger, "for they will be like four children to you."

"What do you mean?" asked the old woman. "How can I sing a gourd to sleep or give it love? How can it help me with my daily chores?"

"Trust me," said the messenger, "for I am sent by the spirit of the mountain."

The Old Widow Woman blinked, and the messenger was gone. She was a great believer in the spirit and prayed to him everyday . . . but what had the stranger meant?

She went out to pick her next four gourds. One of them was the biggest and best and plumpest gourd she had grown in many a year.

The Old Widow Woman remembered the messenger's words. But they still made little sense to her. Gourds were vegetables . . . and how could vegetables be her children? She began to wonder whether she had dreamed the whole thing—or whether it had been one of the villagers playing a mean trick on an old lady.

The best place to dry out her newly picked gourds was in the rafters of her tiny house. It was easy enough to lift the first three gourds into the rafters, but the fourth one—the great big, plump one—was just too big and too heavy for her to lift. So she left it by the fire.

When the Old Widow Woman was away at the market the next day, the mysterious messenger came into her house and touched the four gourds in turn. He started with the big one by the fire and then touched the three in the rafters. The minute he touched the gourds, they turned into children. Then he was gone.

The three children up in the rafters looked down and decided it was too far to jump. "Lift us down, eldest brother," they called out to the largest child—who had been the largest gourd by the fire. They called him "eldest," because they knew the messenger had touched him first.

The eldest brother lifted down the other three, who were soon running around the Old Widow Woman's house, laughing and playing and squealing with delight.

Then the three decided that it was time to do some housework. They fetched, they carried, they tidied and cleaned. The eldest brother sat smiling as he watched them. He was different from the others. He was not as clever, but he played an important role—when the work was done, he lifted the other three children back into the rafters and then settled back down by the fire.

When the Old Widow Woman returned from the market, she found her house cleaner and tidier than it had been in years, and there was a fresh supply of firewood by the door. She couldn't make sense of it. She glanced at the four gourds but thought nothing more of them than what good calabashes they might make.

The next day, when she was at her fruit and vegetable patch, one of the friendlier villagers came up to the Old Widow Woman.

"Who were those children laughing and running and working and playing in and around your house yesterday?" she asked.

"Children?" said the Old Widow Woman. "I don't know anything about any children. How many were there?"

"Three that I saw," replied the villager, "but they moved around in such a whirlwind that it seemed as if there were 20 of them."

The Old Widow Woman began to wonder whether it really had been a messenger from the spirit of the mountain who had visited her—after all, she did pray to him every day—so she crept back to her house to investigate. And there, sure enough, were the three children running around cleaning and tidying, while the eldest brother looked on.

When she stepped into her house, the eldest brother quickly grabbed a child and hung him back up in the rafters, whereupon he turned back into a gourd.

"No! Wait!" she cried. "You are my children, not my servants. I want your help, but I also want to love you and look after you. Don't turn back into gourds. Let me feed you and clothe you, and you can help me in return."

So the gourd in the rafters turned back into a happy child, and his eldest brother lifted him back down onto the floor of the hut.

After that there was always the happy sound of laughter coming from the Old Widow Woman's house or from the fruit and vegetable patch where the children worked. They were such hard workers that they helped grow more fruit and vegetables and make more calabashes than the old woman could ever have done on her own. Soon she had enough money to buy a little more land, and she bought her neighbor's banana trees. Then she had enough to buy a few goats . . . and then enough to buy a whole herd!

Very soon she became a rich farmer and never had to lift a finger to do a day's work.

She never went to the old fruit and vegetable patch any more, but she continued to cook for herself and the children . . . until one day she tripped over the big, plump, eldest boy, who was sitting in his usual place by the fire, grinning a happy grin.

The Rich Old Widow was carrying a pot of stew at the time, and the stew went everywhere. She was furious.

"How many times have I told you not to sit there like a . . . like . . . like the useless vegetable that you are!" she screamed. "I don't know why I bother to cook for you or the other three. You're all just . . . just gourds!"

As the final word passed her lips, the eldest brother turned back into a gourd, and the happy children's voices fell silent. The old widow ran outside, and where, only moments before, three happy, loving children had been tending her garden, there were now three smaller gourds.

Realizing her own foolishness, the Rich Old Widow went back into the house in tears.

The Old Widow lived for many more years and felt even more lonely than before, because having children and losing them was far worse than never having had them in the first place. She died poor, unhappy . . . and alone.

THE LION MAN
AND THE CATTLE

There are myths from all over Africa about lions
that can turn into humans, and humans–usually
medicine men–who can turn into lions.
This myth from Mali is the story of a
lion in human skin.

The herdsmen had had enough. Three of their cows had been killed by a lion in as many days.

"If this carries on, we won't have a herd left," one complained. "What are we to do? We can't move them out of the valley. Perhaps we should call in more men to help us keep watch?"

"Keeping watch won't help," said another. "I can't think of many people who would be willing to put themselves between a hungry lion and its prey."

"I have my spear," said the oldest herdsman.

"And if you come face to face with the lion, you'll shake so much you'll be lucky if you don't spear your own foot!" said the youngest.

They all laughed at this, but the worry about the lion showed in their faces. They decided to go to the medicine man in the next village to see if he knew any spells or had any charms that they could use to protect their herd from the lion.

The medicine man came to their camp in the valley to look at the cattle. "I should be able to protect them for about a month," he said, "but this is expensive magic and will cost you dearly."

"How much?" asked one of the herdsmen.

The medicine man pointed to the biggest, fattest cow in the herd. "That much," he said.

"But that is our most prized cow," said the herdsman.

"And tomorrow the beast may kill that very cow and more besides," the medicine man pointed out.

The herdsmen huddled in a little group and discussed the medicine man's terms. "Very well," said the oldest herdsman at last. "We will give you the biggest, fattest cow if you use your magic to protect our herd from the lion for a month."

So the medicine man took out his charms and spoke his magic words around the herd of cattle. When he was done, he took his payment—the biggest, fattest cow—and led it back to his village.

The herdsmen watched him go. "It's a strange lion that hunts and kills for three days in a row," said one.

"Perhaps it has a large pride to feed," suggested another.

"Perhaps it is no ordinary lion," said the oldest herdsman, his eyes firmly fixed on the medicine man's back.

That night the medicine man led the cow into his home and had a huge feast. The villagers heard the tearing of flesh and the crunching of bones, but had no idea where the sounds were coming from.

Whatever the medicine man had done, it seemed to have worked. For a whole month the cattle grazed safely in the valley . . . then the lion struck again.

This time the oldest herdsman saw the massive beast—with its huge jaws and golden mane—pick out a cow and drag it to the ground, its enormous claws tearing into the terrified animal's flesh.

He ran down the hillside toward the lion, shouting and waving his spear in the hope that he might frighten it off. But the lion ignored him. It bit the back of the cow's neck until the poor, terrified creature stopped thrashing about. Then he dragged it off out of sight.

The other herdsmen heard the old man's cries, but when they arrived, the lion and its prey were nowhere to be seen.

"I think we should pay the medicine man to weave some more of his magic," said the youngest herdsman. "We are no match for this lion. I'm not sure even a gun would frighten him, not that we have one anyway."

So the medicine man came out to the herdsmen's camp once more, and they took him to see the herd.

"So my magic worked for you last time?" he asked.

"Oh, yes," they said. "Could you protect the herd for another month, or perhaps longer still?"

"I can protect your cattle for three months at a time, but no more," said the medicine man. "I have to use strong and expensive magic to protect your herd against such a beast."

"Then we will gladly pay you three cows—"

"Three of your *biggest, fattest* cows," insisted the medicine man.

"Agreed," said a herdsman, "but we can't give them to you today. We'll bring them down to your village for you. We give you our word."

"Very well," said the medicine man, and he performed a magic ritual and then went home.

Time passed, and once again the cattle weren't bothered by the lion, but rather than stick to their promise and pay the medicine man, the herdsmen became foolish.

"Perhaps it's a coincidence that the lion hasn't come back," said one. "I heard that a lion was shot by a hunter down by the river last week. Perhaps that's why our cattle haven't been attacked lately."

"Exactly," said another. "I don't see why we should give the medicine man three of our biggest, fattest cows when we don't even know if his magic has anything to do with protecting the herd!"

So they broke their promise and didn't deliver the cows to the medicine man in payment.

When the medicine man found out that the herdsmen had gone back on their word, he flew into a terrible rage—a rage so terrible, in fact, that news of it reached the herdsmen.

"I think we'd better pay him after all," said the oldest herdsman.

"It's too late for that!" said another. "I think we should move camp across the river in case he comes looking for us." And that's exactly what they did.

The furious medicine man arrived at the banks of the Niger River just as the last one of the cattle was halfway across, being urged on by the frantic herdsmen.

"There he is!" said one of the herdsmen, pointing to the river bank.

"Why doesn't he wade across after us?" spluttered another, with fear.

"Because some medicine men lose their magical powers in rivers," explained the old man. "The water washes the magic off them."

"Then we're safe!" laughed another.

"Not for long," said the oldest herdsman. "There are such things as ferries, remember!"

Sure enough, the medicine man was climbing aboard a ferry as they spoke. The ferryman eyed his latest passenger with particular interest as he stepped aboard the boat.

"Why are you in such a hurry?" asked the ferryman.

"Those men have three cows that are rightfully mine," he roared.

"Really?" said the ferryman, steering the boat out into the Niger River. "Are you sure you don't mean you have had some cows that were rightfully theirs?"

"I don't know what you're talking about," said the medicine man.

"Of course you do," said the ferryman, staring at the medicine man. Because he too was not quite what he seemed, the ferryman could see beyond what ordinary people could see. . . .

The ferryman could see that the medicine man had strange, golden eyes. He could see that the medicine man had very pointed teeth. He could see that the medicine man's skin was never still . . . as though there was rippling fur just beneath the surface. He could see that his hair was like a shaggy mane.

As they neared the shore, and the scent of the cattle filled his nostrils, the medicine man let out a roar of satisfaction.

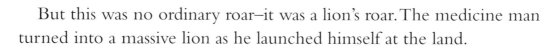

But this was no ordinary roar—it was a lion's roar. The medicine man turned into a massive lion as he launched himself at the land.

"I thought so," said the ferryman. "I can see that someone will have to do something about you."

It happened that the ferryman wasn't just a ferryman. He was also the river chief—a man with powerful magic who brought luck to fishermen, ensured safe crossings in rough waters, and cared for the needs of the people along the riverbank. He knew that no ordinary weapon would kill the lion man. Only two types of weapons could do that—a single copper bullet fired from a gun or a special type of magic arrow.

Having caught and eaten another of the cows, the medicine man now turned back from lion to human and settled himself down for a nap under a tree. What fun he'd had with those herdsmen in the valley! They'd paid him their biggest, fattest cow to protect their cows from him! He smiled to himself, then gave a huge yawn, and went to sleep.

But the lion man was not alone. A hunter who had been tracking him crept into the clearing. The hunter slipped an arrow into his bow and shot it. This lion man wouldn't be bothering any more cattle. You see, the arrow was magic and it ended his days.

MYTHS AND LEGENDS RESOURCES

Here is just a sampling of other resources to look for. These resources on myths and legends are broken down into groups. Enjoy!

GENERAL MYTHOLOGY

The Children's Dictionary of Mythology *edited by David Leeming* (Franklin Watts, 1999). This volume is a dictionary of terms, names, and places in the mythology of various cultures around the world.

Creation Read-aloud Stories from Many Lands *retold by Ann Pilling* (Candlewick Press, 1997). This is a collection of sixteen stories retold in an easy style and presented in three general groups: beginnings, warmth and light, and animals.

The Crystal Pool: Myths and Legends of the World *by Geraldine McCaughrean* (Margaret K. McElderry Books, 1998). Twenty-eight myths and legends from around the world comprise this book. They include the Chinese legend "The Alchemist" and the Celtic legend "Culloch and the Big Pig."

Encyclopedia Mythica
http://www.pantheon.org/areas/mythology/
From this page of the *Encyclopedia Mythica* site you can select from any of five countries to have the mythology of that area displayed.

A Family Treasury of Myths from Around the World *retold by Viviane Koenig* (Abrams, 1998). This collection of ten stories includes myths from Egypt, Africa, Greece, and other places around the world.

Goddesses, Heroes and Shamans: The Young People's Guide to World Mythology *edited by Cynthia O'Neill and others* (Kingfisher, 1994). This book introduces the reader to over five hundred mythological characters from around the world.

Gods, Goddesses and Monsters: An Encyclopedia of World Mythology *retold by Sheila Keenan* (Scholastic, 2000). This beautifully illustrated book discusses the characters and themes of the myths of peoples from Asia to Africa, to North and South America.

The Golden Hoard: Myths and Legends of the World *retold by Geraldine McCaughrean* (Margaret K. McElderry Books, 1995). This book contains twenty-two myths and legends that are exciting, adventurous, magical, and poetic.

The Illustrated Book of Myths: Tales and Legends of the World *retold by Neil Philips* (Dorling Kindersley, 1995). This beautifully illustrated collection brings together many of the most popular of the Greek and Roman, Norse, Celtic, Egyptian, Native American, African, and Indian myths.

Kids Zone: Myths and Fables from Around the World
http://www.afroam.org/children/myths/myths.html
Just click on your choice of the sixteen stories listed, and it will appear in full text.

Legends http://www.planetozkids.com/oban/legends.htm
From this Web page you can get the full text of any of the many listings.

Mythical Birds and Beasts from Many Lands *retold by Margaret Mayo* (Dutton, 1996). This book is a collection of stories that illustrate the special powers of birds and beasts that have become a part of folklore around the world.

Mythology *by Neil Philip* (Alfred A. Knopf, 1999). This superbly illustrated volume from the "Eyewitness Books" series surveys the treatment of such topics as gods and goddesses, the heavens, creation, the elements, and evil as expressed in various mythologies around the world.

Mythology *CD-ROM for Mac and Windows* (Thomas S. Klise, 1996). Educational games and puzzles, a glossary, and a testing section are all part of this CD introduction to Greek and Roman mythology.

Myths and Legends *by Neil Philip* (DK Publishing, 1999). More than fifty myths and legends from around the world are explained through works of art, text, and annotation by one of the world's foremost experts on mythology and folklore.

**The New York Public Library Amazing Mythology:
A Book of Answers for Kids** *by Brendan January*
(John Wiley, 2000). Over two hundred questions and
answers introduce myths from many ancient cultures,
including Egyptian, Greek, Roman, Celtic, Norse, and
Native American.

Plays from Mythology: Grades 4-6 *by L.E. McCullough*
(Smith and Kraus, 1998). Twelve original plays are
included, each with suggestions for staging and costumes.

Sources for Mythology
http://www.best.com/~atta/mythsrcs.html
In addition to defining mythology and distinguishing
it from legend and folklore, this Web site lists primary
sources for myths from many regions of the world,
as well as magazines, dictionaries, and other resources
relating to mythology.

Sun, Moon and Stars *retold by Mary Hoffman*
(Dutton, 1998). More than twenty myths and legends
from around the world, all explaining what was seen
in the sky, make up this exquisitely illustrated book.

AFRICAN

African Gods and their Associates
http://www3.sympatico.ca/untangle/africang.html
This Web page gives you a list of the African gods
with links to further information about them.

African Myths
http://www.cybercomm.net/~grandpa/africanmyths.html
Full text of several tales from the Kenya, Hausa, Ashanti,
and Nyanja tribes are included in this Web site.

Anansi and the Talking Melon *retold by Eric A. Kimmel*
(Holiday House, 1994). Anansi, a legendary character
from Africa, tricks Elephant and some other animals into
thinking that the melon in which he is hiding can talk.

Children's Stories from Africa *4 Video recordings (VHS)*
(Monterey Home Video, 1997). Among the African
Legends on this page: "How the Hare Got His Long
Legs," "How the Porcupine Got His Quills," "The Brave
Sititunga," and "The Greedy Spider."

**The Hero with an African Face: Mythic Wisdom
of Traditional Africa** *by Clyde W. Ford* (Bantam, 2000).
"The Hero with an African Face" is only one of the
several stories included in this book, which also includes
a map of the peoples and myths of Africa and a
pronunciation guide for African words.

Kings, Gods and Spirits from African Mythology
retold by Jan Knappert (Peter Bedrick Books, 1993). This
illustrated collection contains myths and legends of the
peoples of Africa.

Legends of Africa *by Mwizenge Tembo* (Metro Books,
1996). This indexed and illustrated volume is from the
"Myths of the World" series.

Myths and Legends *retold by O. B. Duane* (Brockhampton
Press, 1998). Duane has vividly retold some of the most
gripping African tales.

CELTIC

Celtic Myths *retold by Sam McBratney* (Peter Bedrick,
1997). This collection of fifteen illustrated stories draws
from English, Irish, Scottish, and Welsh folklore.

Excalibur *retold by Hudson Talbott* (Books of Wonder,
1996). In this illustrated story from the legends of King
Arthur, Arthur receives his magical sword, Excalibur

Irish Fairy Tales and Legends *retold by Una Leavy*
(Robert Rinehart, 1996). Cuchulainn, Deirdre, and
Fionn Mac Cumhail are only three of the legendary
characters you will meet in this volume.

Irish Myths and Legends
http://www.mc.maricopa.edu/users/shoemaker/
    Celtic/index.html
This Web site is for those more serious in their
study of Irish myths and legends.

King Arthur *by Rosalind Kerven* (DK Publishing, 1998).
This book from the "Eyewitness Classic" series is a
retelling of the boy who was fated to be the "Once and
Future King" It includes illustrated notes to explain the
historical background of the story.

Robin Hood and His Merry Men *retold by Jane Louise*
Curry (Margaret K. McElderry, 1994). This collection
contains seven short stories of the legendary hero
Robin Hood, who lived with his band of followers in
Sherwood Forest.

**The World of King Arthur and his Court: People,
Places, Legend and Love** *by Kevin Crossley-Holland*
(Dutton, 1998). The author combines legend, anecdote,
fact, and speculation to help answer some of the questions regarding King Arthur and his chivalrous world.

CHINESE

Asian Mythology *by Rachel Storm* (Lorenz, 2000).
Included in this volume are myths and legends of China.

Chinese Culture
http://chineseculture.about.com/culture/
    chineseculture/msub82.htm
Use this Web page as a starting point for further
exploration about Chinese myths and legends.

Chinese Mythology by *Anne Birrell* (Johns Hopkins, 1999). This comprehensive introduction to Chinese mythology will meet the needs of the more serious and the general reader

Chinese Myths and Legends *retold by O. B. Duane and others* (Brockhampton Press, 1998). Introductory notes by the author give further explanation of the thirty-eight stories included in this illustrated volume.

Dragons and Demons by *Stewart Ross* (Cooper Beech, 1998). Included in this collection of myths and legends from Asia are the Chinese myths "Chang Lung the Dragon" and "The Ugly Scholar."

Dragons, Gods and Spirits from Chinese Mythology *retold by Tao Tao Liu Sanders* (Peter Bedrick Books, 1994). The stories in this book include ancient myths about nature, the gods, and creation as well as religious legends.

Fa Mulan: The Story of a Woman Warrior *retold by Robert D. San Souci* (Hyperion, 1998). Artists Jean and Mou-Sien Tseng illustrate this Chinese legend of a young heroine who is courageous, selfless, and wise.

Land of the Dragon: Chinese Myth by *Tony Allan* (Time-Life, 1999). This volume from the "Myth and Mankind" series includes many of China's myths as well as examination of the myth and its historical roots.

Selected Chinese Myths and Fantasies
http://www.chinavista.com/experience/story/story.html
From this Web site and its links you will find several Chinese myths that are enjoyed by children as well as the history of Chinese mythology.

EGYPTIAN

Egyptian Gods and Goddesses by *Henry Barker* (Grosset and Dunlap, 1999). In this book designed for the young reader, religious beliefs of ancient Egypt are discussed, as well as their gods and goddesses.

Egyptian Mythology A-Z: A Young Reader's Companion by *Pat Remler* (Facts on File, 2000). Alphabetically arranged, this resource defines words relating to Egyptian mythology.

Egyptian Myths *retold by Jacqueline Morley* (Peter Bedrick Books, 1999). Legends of the pharaohs, myths about creation, and the search for the secret of all knowledge, make up this illustrated book.

The Gods and Goddesses of Ancient Egypt by *Leonard Everett Fisher* (Holiday House, 1997). This artist/writer describes thirteen of the most important Egyptian gods.

Gods and Myths of Ancient Egypt by *Mary Barnett* (Regency House, 1996). Beautiful color photographs are used to further explain the text in this summary of Egyptian mythology.

Gods and Pharaohs from Egyptian Mythology *retold by Geraldine Harris* (Peter Bedrick Books, 1992). The author gives some background information about the Ancient Egyptians and then retells more than twenty of their myths.

Myth Man's Egyptian Homework Help
http://egyptmyth.com/
Cool Facts and Fun for Kids and *Egyptian Myth Encyclopedia* are only two of the many wonderful links this page will lead you to.

Myths and Civilizations of the Ancient Egyptians by *Sarah Quie* (Peter Bedrick Books, 1998). The author intersperses Egypt's myths with a history of its civilization in this illustrated volume.

The Secret Name of Ra *retold by Anne Rowe* (Rigby Interactive Library, 1996). In this Egyptian myth, Isis tricks Ra into revealing his secret name so that she and her husband Osiris can become rulers of the earth.

Tales from Ancient Egypt *retold by George Hart* (Hoopoe Books, 1994). The seven tales in this collection include stories of animals, of Isis and Horus, of a sailor lost on a magic island, and of pharaohs and their magicians.

Who's Who in Egyptian Mythology by *Anthony S. Mercatante* (Scarecrow Press, 1995). The author has compiled a concise, easy-to-use dictionary of ancient Egyptian deities.

GREEK

Allta and the Queen: A Tale of Ancient Greece by *Priscilla Galloway* (Annick Press, 1995). This made-up story, which is based on Homer's epic poem, *The Odyssey*, reads like a novel.

Cupid and Psyche *retold by M. Charlotte Craft* (Morrow Junior Books, 1996). This classic love story from Greek mythology will appeal to young and old.

Gods and Goddesses by *John Malam* (Peter Bedrick Books, 1999). This volume is packed with information about the important gods and goddesses of ancient Greece, including Zeus, Hera, Athena, and Hades.

Greek and Roman Mythology by *Dan Nardo* (Lucent, 1998). The author examines the historical development of Greco-Roman mythology, its heroes, and its influence on the history of Western civilization.

Guide for Using D'Aulaires' Book of Greek Myths in the Classroom by *Cynthia Ross* (Teacher Created Materials, 1993). This reproducible book includes sample plans, author information, vocabulary-building ideas, cross-curricular activities, quizzes, and many ideas for extending this classic work.

Hercules by *Robert Burleigh* (Harcourt Brace, 1999). Watercolor and color pencil illustrations help to tell the story of Hercules's final labor in which he went back to the underworld and brought back the three-headed dog, Cerberus.

Medusa by *Deborah Nourse Lattimire* (Joanna Cotler Books, 2000). The author/illustrator of this book re-creates the tragedy of one of the best-known Greek myths, the tale of the beautiful Medussa whose conceit causes a curse be placed on her.

The Myths and Legends of Ancient Greece *CD-ROM for Mac and Windows* (Clearvue, 1996). This CD conveys the heroic ideals and spirit of Greek mythology as it follows ten of the best-known myths.

Mythweb http://www.mythweb.com/ This Web page provides links to Greek gods, heroes, an encyclopedia of mythology, and teacher resources.

Pegasus, the Flying Horse *retold by Jane Yolen* (Dutton, 1998). This Greek myth tells of how Bellerophon, with the help of Athena, tames the winged horse Pegasus and conquers the monstrous Chimaera.

The Race of the Golden Apples *retold by Claire Martin* (Dial, 1991). Caldecott Medal winners Leo and Diane Dillon have illustrated this myth of Atalanta, the beautiful Greek princess.

The Random House Book of Greek Myths by *Joan D. Vinge* (Random House, 1999). The author retells some of the famous Greek myths about gods, goddesses, humans, heroes, and monsters, explaining the background of the tales and why these tales have survived.

The Robber Baby: Stories from the Greek Myths *retold by Anne Rockwell* (Greenwillow Books, 1994). Anne Rockwell, a well-known name in children's literature, has put together a superbly retold collection of myths that will be enjoyed by readers of all ages.

NORSE

Beowulf by *Welwyn Wilton Katz* (Groundwood, 2000). The illustrations in this classic legend are based on the art of the Vikings.

Favorite Norse Myths *retold by Mary Pope Osborne* (Scholastic, 1996). These fourteen tales of Norse gods, goddesses, and giants are based on the oldest written sources of Norse mythology, *Prose Edda* and *Poetic Edda*.

The Giant King by *Rosalind Kerven* (NTC Publishing Group, 1998). Photos of artifacts from the Viking Age illustrate these two stories that are rooted in Norse mythology.

Gods and Heroes from Viking Mythology by *Brian Branston* (Peter Bedrick Books, 1994). This illustrated volume tells the stories of Thor, Balder, King Gylfi, and other Nordic gods and goddesses

Handbook of Norse Mythology by *John Lindow* (Ambcc, 2001). For the advanced reader, this handbook covers the tales, their literary and oral sources, includes an A-to-Z of the key mythological figures, concepts and events, and so much more.

Kids Domain Fact File http://www.kidsdomain.co.uk/teachers/resources/ fact_file_viking_gods_and_goddesses.html This child-centered Web page is a dictionary of Viking gods and goddesses.

Myths and Civilization of the Vikings by *Hazel Martell* (Peter Bedrick, 1998). Each of the nine stories in this book is followed by a non-fiction spread with information about Viking society.

Norse Mythology: The Myths and Legends of the Nordic Gods *retold by Arthur Cotterell* (Lorenz Books, 2000). This encyclopedia of the Nordic peoples' myths and legends is generously illustrated with fine art paintings of the classic stories.

Odins' Family: Myths of the Vikings *retold by Neil Philip* (Orchard Books, 1996). This collection of stories of Odin, the All-father, and the other Viking gods Thor, Tyr, Frigg, and Loer is full of excitement that encompasses both tragedy and comedy.

Stolen Thunder: A Norse Myth *retold by Shirley Climo* (Houghton Mifflin, 1994). This story, beautifully illustrated by Alexander Koshkin, retells the Norse myth about the god of Thunder and the recovery of his magic hammer Mjolnir, from the Frost Giany, Thrym.

NORTH AMERICAN

Buffalo Dance: A Blackfoot Legend *retold by Nancy Can Laan* (Little, Brown and Company, 1993). This illustrated version of the Native North American legend tells of the ritual performed before the buffalo hunt.

The Favorite Uncle Remus *by Joel Chandler Harris* (Houghton Mifflin, 1948). This classic work of literature is a collection of stories about Brer Rabbit, Brer Fox, Brer Tarrypin, and others that were told to the author as he grew up in the South.

Iktomi Loses his Eyes: A Plains Indian Story *retold by Paul Goble* (Orchard Books, 1999). The legendary character Iktomi finds himself in a predicament after losing his eyes when he misuses a magical trick.

The Legend of John Henry *retold by Terry Small* (Doubleday, 1994). This African American legendary character, a steel driver on the railroad, pits his strength and speed against the new steam engine hammer that is putting men out of jobs.

The Legend of the White Buffalo Woman *retold by Paul Goble* (National Geographic Society, 1998). This Native American Plains legend tells the story of the White Buffalo Woman who gave her people the Sacred Calf Pipe so that people would pray and commune with the Great Spirit.

Myths and Legends for American Indian Youth http://www.kstrom.net/isk/stories/myths.html Stories from Native Americans across the United States are included in these pages.

Snail Girl Brings Water: a Navajo Story *retold by Geri Keams* (Rising Moon, 1998). This retelling of a traditional Navajo re-creation myth explains how water came to earth.

The Woman Who Fell from the Sky: The Iroquois Story of Creation *retold by John Bierhirst* (William Morrow, 1993). This myth describes how the creation of the world was begun by a woman who fell down to earth from the sky country, and how it was finished by her two sons.

SOUTH AMERICAN (INCLUDING CENTRAL AMERICAN)

Gods and Goddesses of the Ancient Maya *by Leonard Everett Fisher* (Holiday House, 1999). With text and illustration inspired by the art, glyphs, and sculpture of the ancient Maya, this artist and author describes twelve of the most important Maya gods.

How Music Came to the World: An Ancient Mexican Myth *retold by Hal Ober* (Houghton Mifflin, 1994). This illustrated book, which includes author notes and a pronunciation guide, is an Aztec pourquoi story that explains how music came to the world.

Llama and the Great Flood *retold by Ellen Alexander* (Thomas Y. Crowell, 1989). In this illustrated retelling of the Peruvian myth about the Great Flood, a llama warns his master of the coming destruction and leads him and his family to refuge on a high peak in the Andes.

The Legend of the Poinsettia *retold by Tomie dePaola* (G. P. Putnam's Sons,1994). This beautifully illustrated Mexican legend tells of how the poinsettia came to be when a young girl offered her gift to the Christ child.

Lost Realms of Gold: South American Myth *edited by Tony Allan* (Time-Life Books, 2000). This volume, which captures the South American mythmakers' fascination with magic, includes the tale of the first Inca who built the city of Cuzco, as well as the story of the sky people who discovered the rain forest.

People of Corn: A Mayan Story *retold by Mary-Joan Gerson* (Little, Brown, 1995). In this richly illustrated creation story, the gods first try and fail, then try and fail again before they finally succeed.

Tales from the Rain Forest: Myths and Legends from the Amazonian Indians of Brazil *retold by Mercedes Dorson* (Ecco Press, 1997). Ten stories from this region include "The Origin of Rain" and "How the Stars Came to Be."

WHO'S WHO IN MYTHS AND LEGENDS

This is a cumulative listing of some important characters found in all eight volumes of the **World Book Myths and Legends** series.

A

Aegir (EE jihr), also called Hler, was the god of the sea and the husband of Ran in Norse myths. He was lord of the undersea world where drowned sailors spent their days.

Amma (ahm mah) was the creator of the world in the myths of the Dogon people of Africa. Mother Earth was his wife, and Water and Light were his children. Amma also created the people of the world.

Amun (AH muhn), later Amun-Ra, became the king of gods in later Egyptian myths. Still later he was seen as another form of Ra.

Anubis (uh NOO bihs) in ancient Egypt was the god of the dead and helper to Osiris. He had the head of a jackal.

Ao (ow) was a giant turtle in a Chinese myth. He saved the life of Kui.

Aphrodite (af ruh DY tee) in ancient Greece was the goddess of love. She was known for her beauty. The Romans called her Venus.

Arianrod (air YAN rohd) in Welsh legends was the mother of the hero Llew.

Arthur (AHR thur) in ancient Britain was the king of the Britons. He probably was a real person who ruled long before the age of knights in armor. His queen was Guinevere.

Athena (uh THEE nuh) in ancient Greece was the goddess of war. The Romans called her Minerva.

Atum (AH tuhm) was the creator god of ancient Egypt and the father of Shu and Tefnut. He later became Ra-Atum.

B

Babe (bayb) in North American myths was the big blue ox owned by Paul Bunyan.

Balder (BAWL dur) was the god of light in Norse myths. He was the most handsome of all gods and was Frigga's favorite son.

Balor (BAL awr) was an ancient chieftain in Celtic myths who had an evil eye. He fought Lug, the High King of Ireland.

Ban Hu (bahn hoo) was the dog god in a myth that tells how the Year of the Dog in the Chinese calendar got its name.

Bastet (BAS teht), sometimes Bast (bast) in ancient Egypt was the mother goddess. She was often shown as a cat. Bastet was the daughter of Ra and the sister of Hathor and Sekhmet.

Bellerophon (buh LEHR uh fahn) in ancient Greek myths was a hero who captured and rode the winged horse, Pegasus.

Blodeuwedd was the wife of Llew in Welsh legends. She was made of flowers woven together by magic.

Botoque (boh toh kay) in Kayapó myths was the boy who first ate cooked meat and told people about fire.

Brer Rabbit (brair RAB iht) was a clever trickster rabbit in North American myths.

C

Chameleon (kuh MEEL yuhn) in a Yoruba myth of Africa was a messenger sent to trick the god Olokun and teach him a lesson.

Conchobar (KAHN koh bahr), also called Conor, was the king of Ulster. He was a villain in many Irish myths.

Coyote (ky OH tee) was an evil god in myths of the Maidu and some other Native American people.

Crow (kroh) in Inuit myths was the wise bird who brought daylight to the Inuit people.

Cuchulain (koo KUHL ihn), also Cuchullain or Cuchulan, in Irish myths was Ireland's greatest warrior of all time. He was the son of Lug and Dechtire.

Culan (KOO luhn) in Irish myths was a blacksmith. His hound was killed by Setanta, who later became Cuchulain.

D

Davy Crockett (DAY vee KRAHK iht) was a real person. He is remembered as an American frontier hero who died in battle and also in legends as a great hunter and woodsman.

Dechtire (DEHK teer) in Irish myths was the sister of King Conchobar and mother of Cuchulain.

Deirdre (DAIR dray) in Irish myths was the daughter of Fedlimid. She refused to wed Conchobar. It was said that she would lead to Ireland's ruin.

Di Jun (dee joon) was god of the Eastern Sky in Chinese myths. He lived in a giant mulberry tree.

Di Zang Wang (dee zahng wahng) in Chinese myths was a Buddhist monk who was given that name when he became the lord of the underworld. His helper was Yan Wang, god of the dead.

Dionysus (dy uh NY suhs) was the god of wine in ancient Greek myths. He carried a staff wrapped in vines.

Dolapo was the wife of Kigbo in a Yoruba myth of Africa.

E

Eight Immortals (ihm MAWR tuhlz) in Chinese myths were eight ordinary human beings whose good deeds led them to truth and enlightenment. The Eight Immortals were godlike heroes. They had special powers to help people.

El Niño (ehl NEEN yoh) in Inca myths was the ruler of the wind, the weather, and the ocean and its creatures.

Emer (AYV ur) in Irish myths was the daughter of Forgal the Wily and wife of Cuchulain.

F

Fafnir (FAHV nihr) in Norse myths was a son of Hreidmar. He killed his father for his treasure, sent his brother Regin away, and turned himself into a dragon.

Frey (fray), also called Freyr, was the god of summer in Norse myths. His chariot was pulled by a huge wild boar.

Freya (FRAY uh) was the goddess of beauty and love in Norse myths. Her chariot was pulled by two large cats.

Frigga (FRIHG uh), also called Frigg, in Norse myths was the wife of Odin and mother of many gods. She was the most powerful goddess in Asgard.

Frog was an animal prince in an Alur myth of Africa. He and his brother, Lizard, competed for the right to inherit the throne of their father.

Fu Xi (foo shee) in a Chinese myth was a boy who, with his sister Nü Wa, freed the Thunder God and was rewarded. His name means Gourd Boy.

G

Gaunab was Death, who took on a human form in a Khoi myth of Africa. Tsui'goab fought with Gaunab to save his people.

Geb (gehb) in ancient Egypt was the Earth itself. All plants and trees grew from his back. He was the brother and husband of Nut and the father of the gods Osiris, Isis, Seth, and Nephthys.

Glooscap (glohs kap) was a brave and cunning god in the myths of Algonquian Native American people. He was a trickster who sometimes got tricked.

Guinevere (GWIHN uh vihr) in British and Welsh legends was King Arthur's queen, who was also loved by Sir Lancelot.

Gwydion (GWIHD ih uhn) in Welsh legends was the father of Llew and the nephew of the magician and ruler, Math.

H

Hades (HAY deez) in ancient Greece was the god of the dead. Hades was also called Pluto (PLOO toh). The Romans called him Dis.

Hairy Man was a frightening monster in African American folk tales.

Harpy (HAHRP ee) was one of the hideous winged women in Greek myths. The hero Jason and his Argonauts freed King Phineas from the harpies' power.

Hathor (HATH awr) was worshiped in the form of a cow in ancient Egypt, but she also appeared as an angry lioness. She was the daughter of Ra and the sister of Bastet and Sekhmet.

Heimdall (HAYM dahl) was the god in Norse myths who guarded the rainbow bridge joining Asgard, the home of the gods, to other worlds.

Hel (hehl), also called Hela, was the goddess of death in Norse myths. The lower half of her body was like a rotting corpse. Hel was Loki's daughter.

Helen (HEHL uhn), called Helen of Troy, was a real person in ancient Greece. According to legend, she was known as the most beautiful woman in the world. Her capture by Paris led to the Trojan War.

Heng E (huhng ay), sometimes called Chang E, was a woman in Chinese myths who became the moon goddess. She was the wife of Yi the Archer.

Hera (HEHR uh) in ancient Greece was the queen of heaven and the wife of Zeus. The Romans called her Juno.

Heracles (HEHR uh kleez) in ancient Greek myths was a hero of great strength. He was the son of Zeus. He had to complete twelve tremendous tasks in order to become one of the gods. The Romans called him Hercules.

Hermes (HUR meez) was the messenger of the gods in Greek myths. He wore winged sandals. The Romans called him Mercury.

Hoder (HOO dur) was Balder's twin brother in Norse myths. He was blind. It was said that after a mighty battle he and Balder would be born again.

Hoenir (HAY nihr), also called Honir, was a god in Norse myths. In some early myths, he is said to be Odin's brother.

Horus (HAWR uhs) in ancient Egypt was the son of Isis and Osiris. He was often shown with the head of a falcon. Horus fought Seth to rule Egypt.

Hreidmar (HRAYD mahr) was a dwarf king in Norse myths who held Odin for a huge pile of treasure. His sons were Otter, Fafnir, and Regin.

Hyrrokkin (HEER rahk kihn) in Norse myths was a terrifying female giant who rode an enormous wolf using poisonous snakes for reins.

I

Irin-Mage (eereen mah geh) in Tupinambá myths was the only person to be saved when the creator, Monan, destroyed the other humans. Irin-Mage became the ancestor of all people living today.

Isis (EYE sihs) in ancient Egypt was the goddess of fertility and a master of magic. She became the most powerful of all the gods and goddesses. She was the sister and wife of Osiris and mother of Horus.

J

Jade Emperor (jayd EHM puhr uhr) in Buddhist myths of China was the chief god in Heaven.

Jason (JAY suhn) was a hero in Greek myths. His ship was the Argo, and the men who sailed with him on his adventures were called the Argonauts.

Johnny Appleseed (AP uhl seed) was a real person, John Chapman. He is remembered in legends as the person who traveled across North America, planting apple orchards.

K

Kaboi (kah boy) was a very wise man in a Carajá myth. He helped his people find their way from their underground home to the surface of the earth.

Kewawkwuí (kay wow kwoo) were a group of powerful, frightening giants and magicians in the myths of Algonquian Native American people.

Kigbo (keeg boh) was a stubborn man in a Yoruba myth of Africa. His stubbornness got him into trouble with spirits.

Kodoyanpe (koh doh yahn pay) was a good god in the myths of the Maidu and some other Native American people. He was the brother of the evil god Coyote.

Kuang Zi Lian (kwahng dsee lee ehn) in a Taoist myth of China was a very rich, greedy farmer who was punished by one of the Eight Immortals.

Kui in Chinese myths was an ugly, brilliant scholar who became God of Examinations.

Kvasir (KVAH sihr) in Norse myths was the wisest of all the gods in Asgard.

L

Lancelot (lan suh laht) in British and Welsh legends was King Arthur's friend and greatest knight. He was secretly in love with Guinevere.

Lao Zi (low dzuh) was the man who founded the Chinese religion of Taoism. He wrote down the Taoist beliefs in a book, the *Tao Te Ching*.

Li Xuan (lee shwahn) was one of the Eight Immortals in ancient Chinese myths.

Light (lyt) was a child of Amma, the creator of the world, in a myth of the Dogon people of Africa.

Lizard (LIHZ urd) was an animal prince in an Alur myth of Africa. He was certain that he, and not his brother, Frog, would inherit the throne of their father.

Llew Llaw Gyffes (LE yoo HLA yoo GUHF ehs), also Lleu Law Gyffes, was a hero in Welsh myths who had many adventures. His mother was Arianrod and his father was Gwydion.

Loki (LOH kee) in Norse myths was a master trickster. His friends were Odin and Thor. Loki was half giant and half god, and could be funny and also cruel. He caused the death of Balder.

Lord of Heaven was the chief god in some ancient Chinese myths.

Lug (luk) in Irish myths was the Immortal High King of Ireland, Master of All Arts.

M

Maira-Monan (mah ee rah moh nahn) was the most powerful son of Irin-Mage in Tupinambá myths. He was destroyed by people who were afraid of his powers.

Manco Capac (mahn kih kah pahk) in Inca myths was the founder of the Inca people. He was one of four brothers and four sisters who led the Inca to their homeland.

Manitou (MAN ih toh) was the greatest and most powerful of all gods in Native American myths of the Iroquois people.

Math (mohth) in Welsh myths was a magician who ruled the Welsh kingdom of Gwynedd.

Michabo (mee chah boh) in the myths of Algonquian Native American people was the Great Hare, who taught people to hunt and brought them luck. He was a son of West Wind.

Monan (moh nahn) was the creator in Tupinambá myths.

Monkey (MUNG kee) is the hero of many Chinese stories. The most cunning of all monkeys, he became the king of monkeys and caused great troubles for the gods.

N

Nanook (na NOOK) was the white bear in myths of the Inuit people.

Naoise (NEE see) in Irish myths was Conchobar's nephew and the lover of Deirdre. He was the son of Usnech and brother of Ardan and Ainle.

Nekumonta (neh koo mohn tah) in Native American myths of the Iroquois people was a person whose goodness helped him save his people from a terrible sickness.

Nü Wa (nyuh wah) in a Chinese myth was a girl who, with her brother, Fu Xi, freed the Thunder God and was rewarded. Her name means Gourd Girl.

Nuada (NOO uh thuh) in Irish myths was King of the Tuatha Dé Danann, the rulers of all Ireland. He had a silver hand.

O

Odin (OH dihn), also called Woden, in Norse myths was the chief of all the gods and a brave warrior. He had only one eye. He was the husband of Frigga and father of many of the gods. His two advisers were the ravens Hugin and Munin.

Odysseus (oh DIHS ee uhs) was a Greek hero who fought in the Trojan War. The poet Homer wrote of his many adventures.

Oedipus (ED uh puhs) was a tragic hero in Greek myths. He unknowingly killed his own father and married his mother.

Olodumare (oh loh doo mah ray) was the supreme god in Yoruba myths of Africa.

Olokun (oh loh koon) was the god of water and giver of life in Yoruba myths of Africa. He challenged Olodumare for the right to rule.

Orpheus (AWR fee uhs) in Greek myths was famed for his music. He followed his wife, Euridice, to the kingdom of the dead to plead for her life.

Osiris (oh SY rihs) in ancient Egypt was the ruler of the dead in the kingdom of the West. He was the brother and husband of Isis and the father of Horus.

P

Pamola (pah moh lah) in the myths of Algonquian Native American people was an evil spirit of the night.

Pan Gu (pahn goo) in Chinese myths was the giant who was the first living being.

Pandora (pan DAWR uh) in ancient Greek myths was the first woman.

Paris (PAR ihs) was a real person, a hero from the city of Troy. He captured Helen, the queen of a Greek kingdom, and took her to Troy.

Paul Bunyan (pawl BUHN yuhn) was a tremendously strong giant lumberjack in North American myths.

Perseus (PUR see uhs) was a human hero in myths of ancient Greece. His most famous adventure was killing Medusa, a creature who turned anyone who looked at her to stone.

Poseidon (puh SY duhn) was the god of the sea in myths of ancient Greece. He carried a three-pronged spear called a trident to make storms and control the waves. The Romans called him Neptune.

Prometheus (pruh MEE thee uhs) was the cleverest of the gods in Greek myths. He was a friend to humankind.

Q

Queen Mother of the West was a goddess in Chinese myths.

R

Ra (rah), sometimes Re (ray), was the sun god of ancient Egypt. He was often shown with the head of a hawk. Re became the most important god. Other gods were sometimes combined with him and had Ra added to their names.

Ran (rahn) was the goddess of the sea in Norse myths. She pulled sailors from their boats in a large net and dragged them underwater.

Red Jacket in Chinese myths was an assistant to Wen Chang, the god of literature. His job was to help students who hadn't worked very hard.

S

Sekhmet (SEHK meht) in ancient Egypt was a bloodthirsty goddess with the head of a lioness. She was the daughter of Ra and the sister of Bastet and Hathor.

Setanta in Irish myths was Cuchulain's name before he killed the hound of Culan.

Seth (set), sometimes Set, in ancient Egypt was the god of chaos and confusion, who fought Horus to rule Egypt. He was the evil son of Geb and Nut.

Shanewis (shah nay wihs) in Native American myths of the Iroquois people was the wife of Nekumonta.

Shu (shoo) in ancient Egypt was the father of the sky goddess Nut. He held Nut above Geb, the Earth, to keep the two apart.

Sinchi Roca was the second emperor of the Inca. According to legend, he was the son of Ayar Manco (later known as Manco Capac) and his sister Mama Ocllo.

Skirnir (SKEER nihr) in Norse myths was a brave, faithful servant of the god Frey.

Sphinx (sfihngks) in Greek myths was a creature that was half lion and half woman, with eagle wings. It killed anyone who failed to answer its riddle.

T

Tefnut (TEHF noot) was the moon goddess in ancient Egypt. She was the sister and wife of Shu and the mother of Nut and Geb.

Theseus (THEE see uhs) was a human hero in myths of ancient Greece. He killed the Minotaur, a half-human, half-bull creature, and freed its victims.

Thor (thawr) was the god of thunder in Norse myths. He crossed the skies in a chariot pulled by goats and had a hammer, Mjollnir, and a belt, Meginjardir.

Thunder God (THUN dur gahd) in Chinese myths was the god of thunder and rain. He got his power from water and was powerless if he could not drink.

Tsui'goab (tsoo ee goh ahb) was the god of rain in myths of the Khoi people of Africa. He was a human who became a god after he fought to save his people.

Tupan (too pahn) was the spirit of thunder and lightning in Inca myths.

Tyr (tihr) was the god of war in Norse myths. He was the bravest god and was honorable and true, as well. He had just one hand.

U

Utgard-Loki (OOT gahrd LOH kee) in Norse myths was the clever, crafty giant king of Utgard. He once disguised himself as a giant called Skrymir to teach Thor a lesson.

W

Water God (WAW tur gahd) in Chinese myths was a god who sent rain and caused floods.

Wen Chang (wehn chuhng) in Chinese myths was the god of literature. His assistants were Kui and Red Jacket.

Wu (woo) was a lowly courtier in a Chinese myth who fell in love with a princess.

X

Xi He (shee heh) in Chinese myths was the goddess wife of Di Jun, the god of the eastern sky.

Xiwangmu (shee wahng moo) in Chinese myths was the owner of the Garden of Immortal Peaches.

Xuan Zang (shwahn dsahng), also called Tripitaka, was a real person, a Chinese Buddhist monk who traveled to India to gather copies of religious writings. Legends about him tell that Monkey was his traveling companion.

Y

Yan Wang (yahn wahng) was the god of the dead and judge of the first court of the Underworld in Chinese myths. He was helper to Di Zang Wang.

Yao (yow) was a virtuous emperor in Chinese myths. Because Yao lived simply and was a good leader, Yi the Archer was sent to help him.

Yi (yee) was an archer in Chinese myths who was sent by Di Jun to save the earth, in answer to Yao's prayers.

Z

Zeus (zoos) in ancient Greece was the king of gods and the god of thunder and lightning. The Romans called him Jupiter.

Zhao Shen Xiao (zhow shehn shi ow) in Chinese myths was a good magistrate, or official, who arrested the greedy merchant Kuang Zi Lian.

MYTHS AND LEGENDS GLOSSARY

This is a cumulative glossary of some important places and terms found in all eight volumes of the *World Book Myths and Legends* series.

A

Alfheim (AHLF hym) in Norse myth was the home of the light elves.

Asgard (AS gahrd) in Norse myths was the home of the warrior gods who were called the Aesir. It was connected to the earth by a rainbow bridge.

Augean (aw JEE uhn) stables were stables that the Greek hero Heracles had to clean as one of his twelve labors. He made the waters of two rivers flow through the stables and wash away the filth.

Avalon (AV uh lahn) in British legends was the island where King Arthur was carried after he died in battle. The legend says he will rise again to lead Britain.

B

Bard (bahrd) was a Celtic poet and singer in ancient times. A bard entertained people by making up and singing poems about brave deeds.

Battle of the Alamo (AL uh moh) was a battle between Texas settlers and Mexican forces when Texas was fighting for independence from Mexico. It took place at the Alamo, a fort in San Antonio, in 1836.

Bifrost (BEE fruhst) in Norse myths was a rainbow bridge that connected Asgard with the world of people.

Black Land in ancient Egypt was the area of fertile soil around the banks of the River Nile. Most people lived there.

Brer Rabbit (brair RAB iht) myths are African American stories about a rabbit who played tricks on his friends. The stories grew out of animal myths from Africa.

C

Canoe Mountain in a Maidu myth of North America was the mountain on which the evil Coyote took refuge from a flood sent to drown him.

Changeling (CHAYNG lihng) in Celtic myths was a fairy child who had been swapped with a human baby at birth. Changelings were usually lazy and clumsy.

Confucianism (kuhn FYOO shuhn IHZ uhm) is a Chinese way of life and religion. It is based on the teachings of Confucius, also known as Kong Fu Zi, and is more than 2,000 years old.

Creation myths (kree AY shuhn mihths) are myths that tell how the world began.

D

Dwarfs (dwawrfs) in Norse myths were small people of great power. They were skilled at making tools and weapons.

F

Fairies (FAIR eez) in Celtic myths were called the Little People. They are especially common in Irish legends, where they are called leprechauns.

Fomors (FOH wawrz) in Irish myths were hideous giants who invaded Ireland and were fought by Lug.

G

Giants (JY uhnts) in Norse myths were huge people who had great strength and great powers. They often struggled with the warrior gods of Asgard.

Gnome (nohm) was a small, odd-looking person in the myths of many civilizations. In Inca myths, for example, gnomes were tiny people with very big beards.

Golden Apples of the Hesperides (heh SPEHR uh deez) were apples of gold in a garden that only the Greek gods could enter. They were collected by the hero Heracles as one of his twelve labors.

Golden fleece was the fleece of a ram that the Greek hero Jason won after many adventures with his ship, Argo, and his companion sailors, the Argonauts.

Green Knoll (nohl) was the home of the Little People, or fairies, in Irish and Scottish myths.

J

Jotunheim (YUR toon hym) in Norse myths was the land of the giants.

L

Lion men in myths of Africa were humans who can turn themselves into lions.

Little People in Celtic legends and folk tales are fairies. They are often fine sword makers and blacksmiths.

M

Machu Picchu (MAH choo PEE choo) is the ruins of an ancient city built by the Inca in the Andes Mountains of Peru.

Medecolin (may day coh leen) were a tribe of evil sorcerers in the myths of Algonquian Native American people.

Medicine (MEHD uh sihn) **man** is a wise man or shaman who has special powers. Medicine men also appear as beings with special powers in myths of Africa and North and South America. Also see **Shaman.**

Midgard (MIHD gahrd) in Norse myths was the world of people.

Muspell (MOOS pehl) in Norse myths was part of the Underworld. It was a place of fire.

N

Nidavellir in Norse myths was the land of the dwarfs.

Niflheim in Norse myths was part of the Underworld. It included Hel, the kingdom of the dead.

Nirvana (nur VAH nuh) in the religion of Buddhism is a state of happiness that people find when they have freed themselves from wanting things. People who reach Nirvana no longer have to be reborn.

O

Oracle (AWRR uh kuhl) in ancient Greece was a sacred place served by people who could foretell the future. Greeks journeyed there to ask questions about their fortunes. Also see **Soothsayer.**

P

Pacariqtambo (pahk kah ree TAHM boh) in Inca myths was a place of three caves from which the first people stepped out into the world. It is also called Paccari Tampu.

Poppykettle was a clay kettle made for brewing poppy-seed tea. In an Inca myth, a poppykettle was used for a boat.

Prophecy (PRAH feh see) is a prediction made by someone who foretells the future.

R

Ragnarok (RAHG nah ruhk) in Norse myths was the final battle of good and evil, in which the giants would fight against the gods of Asgard.

S

Sahara (sah HAH rah) is a vast desert that covers much of northern Africa.

Seriema was a bird in a Carajá myth of South America whose call led the first people to try to find their way from underground to the surface of the earth.

Shaman (SHAH muhn) can be a real person, a medicine man or wise person who knows the secrets of nature. Shamans also appear as beings with special powers in some myths of North and South America. Also see **Medicine man.**

Soothsayer (sooth SAY ur) in ancient Greece was someone who could see into the future. Also see **Oracle.**

Svartalfheim (SVAHRT uhl hym) in Norse myths was the home of the dark elves.

T

Tar Baby was a sticky doll made of tar used to trap Brer Rabbit, a tricky rabbit in African American folk tales.

Tara (TAH rah) in Irish myths was the high seat, or ruling place, of the Irish kings.

Trickster (TRIHK stur) **animals** are clever ones that appear in many myths of North America, South America, and Africa.

Trojan horse. See **Wooden horse of Troy.**

Tuatha dÈ Danann (THOO uh huh day DUH nuhn) were the people of the goddess Danu. Later they were known as gods of Ireland themselves.

V

Vanaheim (VAH nah hym) in Norse myths was the home of the fertility gods.

W

Wadjet eye was a symbol used by the people of ancient Egypt. It stood for the eye of the gods Ra and Horus and was supposed to bring luck.

Wheel of Transmigration (tranz my GRAY shuhn) in the religion of Buddhism is the wheel people's souls reach after they die. From there they are sent back to earth to be born into a higher or lower life.

Wooden horse of Troy was a giant wooden horse built by the Greeks during the Trojan War. The Greeks hid soldiers in the horse's belly and left the horse for the Trojans to find.

Y

Yang (yang) is the male quality of light, sun, heat, and dryness in Chinese beliefs. Yang struggles with Yin for control of things.

Yatkot was a magical tree in an African myth of the Alur people.

Yggdrasil (IHG drah sihl) in Norse myths was a mighty tree that held all three worlds together and reached up into the stars.

Yin (yihn) is the female quality of shadow, moon, cold, and water in Chinese beliefs. Yin struggles with Yang for control of things.

CUMULATIVE INDEX

This is an alphabetical list of important topics covered in all eight volumes of the **World Book Myths and Legends** series. Next to each entry is at least one pair of numbers separated by a slash mark (/). For example, the entry for Argentina is "**Argentina 8/4**". The first number tells you what volume to look in for information. The second number tells you what page you should turn to in that volume. Sometimes a topic appears in more than one place. When it does, additional volume and page numbers are given. Here's a reminder of the volume numbers and titles: 1, *African Myths and Legends;* 2, *Ancient Egyptian Myths and Legends;* 3, *Ancient Greek Myths and Legends;* 4, *Celtic Myths and Legends;* 5, *Chinese Myths and Legends;* 6, *Norse Myths and Legends;* 7, *North American Myths and Legends;* 8, *South American Myths and Legends.*

For information on other World Book products, visit our Web site at www.worldbook.com or call 1-800-WORLDBK (967-5325).

For information on sales to schools and libraries, call 1-800-975-3250.

Cover background illustration by Paul Perreault

Pages 48-64: ©2002 World Book, Inc. All rights reserved. WORLD BOOK and the GLOBE DEVICE are registered trademarks or trademarks of World Book, Inc. No part of this publication may be reproduced, stored in a retrieval system, or transmitted in any form or by any means electronic, mechanical, photocopying, recording, or otherwise, without prior written permission from the publisher.

World Book, Inc.
233 North Michigan Avenue
Chicago, IL 60601

Pages 1–47: format and illustrations, ©1997 Belitha Press; text, ©1997 Philip Ardagh

Printed in Hong Kong
2 3 4 5 6 7 8 9 10 10 09 08 07 06 05 04 03 02

ISBN(set): 0-7166-2613-6
African Myths and Legends
ISBN: 0-7166-2605-5
LC: 2001026492
Ancient Egyptian Myths and Legends
ISBN: 0-7166-2606-3
LC: 2001026501
Ancient Greek Myths and Legends
ISBN: 0-7166-2607-1
LC: 2001035959
Celtic Myths and Legends
ISBN: 0-7166-2608-X
LC: 20011026496
Chinese Myths and Legends
ISBN: 0-7166-2609-8
LC: 2001026489
Norse Myths and Legends
ISBN: 0-7166-2610-1
LC: 2001026488
North American Myths and Legends
ISBN: 0-7166-2611-X
LC: 2001026490
South American Myths and Legends
ISBN: 0-7166-2612-8
LC: 2001026491